The Effortless S

Cookbook

Pressure Cooker Recipes for Busy People

BY - Zoe Moore

Copyright 2022 by Zoe Moore

Copyright Notes

I've spent a lifetime in the kitchen, and all the knowledge I've accumulated from that hasn't come without its fair share of burns and disasters. Fortunately, I'm a lot wiser from it all and am now in a place where I can share my knowledge and skills with you. However, that doesn't mean anyone can use my content for any purpose they please. This book has been copyrighted as a way to protect my story, knowledge, and recipes, so I can continue sharing them with others into the future.

Do not make any print or electronic reproductions, sell, re-publish, or distribute this book in parts or as a whole unless you have express written consent from me or my team.

This is a condensed version of the copyright license, but it's everything you need to know in a nutshell. Please help protect my life's work and all the burns and melted spatulas I have accumulated in order to publish this book.

Table of Contents

Introduction 5

    Recipe 1 - Carne Guisada 7

    Recipe 2 - Chicken Enchilada Soup 10

    Recipe 3 - Chicken Bog 13

    Recipe 4 - Cooker Fabulous Fajitas 16

    Recipe 5 - Hearty Pork & Black Beans Nachos 19

    Recipe 6 - Pressure Cooker Sauerbraten 22

    Recipe 7 - Red Calm Sauce 25

    Recipe 8 - Chicken with Olives and Artichokes 28

    Recipe 9 - Pork Pozole 31

    Recipe 10 - Carolina Shrimp & Cheddar Grits 34

    Recipe 11 - Brussels Sprouts 37

    Recipe 12 - Cooker Boeuf Bourguignon 39

    Recipe 13 - Chinese Ribs 42

    Recipe 14 - Sausage & Waffle Bake 45

    Recipe 15 - Risotto with Shrimp and Asparagus 48

Recipe 16 - Sweet 'n' Sour Pork 51

Recipe 17 - Tuna Noodles Casserole 54

Recipe 18 - Mustard Pork Roast 57

Recipe 19 - Denver Omelet Frittata 60

Recipe 20 - Cooker Cranberry Apple Grains 63

Recipe 21 - Buffalo Shrimp Mac & Cheese 65

Recipe 22 - Cooker Turkey with Berry Compote 68

Recipe 23 - Apple Pear Compote 71

Recipe 24 - Cooker Mediterranean Chicken Orzo 74

Recipe 25 - Cherry & Spice Rice Pudding 77

Recipe 26 - Cooker Pork Chili Verde 80

Recipe 27 - Memphis Style Ribs 83

Recipe 28 - Cooker Balsamic Chicken and Apple 86

Recipe 29 - Cooker Chicken Thighs in Wine Sauce 89

Recipe 30 - Cooker Cheery – Almond Oatmeal 92

About the Author 94

Author's Afterthoughts 95

Introduction

Just like blenders and toaster ovens were new to the market at one point and revolutionized cooking, pressure cookers are pretty much the same. For some reason though, not everyone has one or trusts them. While there are certain risks involved, we think the benefits outweigh them by far! Besides, as long as you're closing the lid properly and waiting for all the steam to release before opening, what could go wrong?

If you're lucky enough to have a pressure cooker stored somewhere in your garage, it's time to dig it out right now. We don't care if it takes you all week to find it, once it hits the stove, it's never going back there again. That's because we've tasked ourselves with showing you just how wonderful they are. They're easy to clean, perfect for large or small batches, and super easy to use. Besides, they cut cooking time by about 70%! Having said this, why wouldn't you want to use it?

Once it's out, start flipping through our recipes and decide what the week's menu is going to look like. Will it be pozole and beef bourguignon? How about Chinese ribs or Mediterranean chicken orzo? Whatever it is you're craving, the pressure cooker will help you get there within minutes so let's get started! Cooking has never been easier or quicker, just take a leap of faith and trust us. We've done this before.

xxxxxxxxxxxxxxxxxxxxxxxxxxxxxxxxxxxxxxxxxxx

Recipe 1 - Carne Guisada

This recipe is a quick meal, and it's full of nutrition and makes a unique taste. Let's try this recipe and serve it warm to your buddies.

Total Prep Time: 50 min

Yield: 12

List of Ingredients:

- Beer 1 bottle of 12 ounces
- Tomato paste 2 tbsp.
- Chopped and seeded jalapeno pepper 1
- Worcestershire sauce 4 tsp.
- Red wine vinegar 1/2 tsp.
- Bay leaf 1
- Paprika 1/2 tsp.
- Chili powder 2 tsp.
- Ground cumin 1½ tsp.
- Salt 1/2 tsp.
- Minced garlic cloves 2
- Red pepper flakes 2 to 3 tsp.
- Dash liquid spoon optional
- Boneless pork 1 (3 lbs.) 2 inches pieces
- All-purpose flour 1/4 cup
- Chopped onion 1 medium
- Chopped and unpeeled red potatoes 2 large
- Water 1/4 cup
- Tortillas, cooked rice, lime wedges, and minced cilantro (optional)

xxxxxxxxxxxxxxxxxxxxxxxxxxxxxxxxxxxxxxxxx

Procedure:

1. Take an electric pressure cooker in a 6 qt. Mix up the 1 to 13 ingredients, and if you want to add the liquid smoke.

2. Stir it in the onion and pork.

3. Lock the lid in place and cook it on high for 3 minutes more.

4. Allow it naturally to release the pressure for 5 minutes and then quickly release any remaining pressure again.

5. Lock the lid in place and cook it for 5 minutes more.

6. When it becomes finished cooking, allow the pressure cooker to release naturally for 10 minutes.

7. According to manufacturers' instructions, release quickly any of the remaining pressure.

8. Discard all the bay leaves, skim the fat from the juices.

9. Select the sauté setting and adjust it on normal heat; now, bring it to boil.

10. Combine the 1/4 cup of water and the flour. Stir it into the simmering sauce.

11. Cook until it gets thickened and boiling for 1-2 minutes.

12. Shred the pork with the help of two forks, toss it with sauce.

13. Serve it with the remaining ingredients.

14. Serve it warm and enjoy it.

Recipe 2 - Chicken Enchilada Soup

This recipe makes you ready an instant pot of enchilada soup with chicken, and you can serve or garnish it with sour cream, avocado, and tortillas strips.

Total Prep Time: 25 min

Yield: 8

List of Ingredients:

- Canola oil 1 tbsp.
- Anaheim or poblano finely chopped peppers 2
- Chopped onion 1 medium
- Minced garlic cloves 3
- Chicken breast skinless boneless 1 pound
- Chicken broth 1 carton (48 ounces)
- Diced tomatoes Mexican undrained 1 can (14½ ounces)
- Enchilada sauce 1 can (10 ounces)
- Tomato paste 2 tbsp.
- Chili powder 1 tbsp.
- Ground cumin 2 tsp.
- Pepper ½ tsp.
- Chipotle hot pepper sauce 1/2 to 1 tsp.
- Fresh minced cilantro 1/3 cup
- Cheddar shredded cheese cubed, or avocado, tortilla strips, and sour cream optional

xxxxxxxxxxxxxxxxxxxxxxxxxxxxxxxxxxxxxxxxx

Procedure:

1. Take an electric pressure cooker, select the sauté in 6 qt size and adjust it on high heat.

2. Now add the oil. When the oil becomes hot, add the onion and peppers; cook it until tender for 6-8 minutes.

3. Add the garlic and cook it for 1 minute.

4. Add the chicken broth, enchilada sauce, tomatoes, seasoning, and tomato paste. If you want, then add pepper sauce.

5. Lock the lid and make sure the vent is closed.

6. Now select the manual setting and adjust it to high heat for 8 minutes.

7. When it becomes finished cooking, allow the pressure cooker to release the naturally for 7 minutes.

8. Remove the chicken from the pressure cooker.

9. Take two forks and shred the chicken. Return it to the pressure cooker.

10. Stir it in the cilantro.

11. Serve it with the topping you want.

12. Serve it immediately and warm; enjoy it.

Recipe 3 - Chicken Bog

This recipe has an interesting way to present with chicken and rice, it's a simple dish, but in classic taste and texture, you can serve it with different herbs and vegetables or with the remaining sausages.

Total Prep Time: 30 min

Yield: 8

List of Ingredients:

- Canola oil 1 tbsp.
- Chopped onion 1 medium
- Smoked sausages 8 ounces (halved and sliced 1/2 inch)
- Minced garlic cloves 3
- Chicken broth 5 cups
- Uncooked converted rice 2 cups
- Salt 1 tsp.
- Pepper 1 tsp.
- Rotisserie chicken 1 (about 3 lbs.) shredded and meat removed
- Green onion thinly sliced
- Hot sauce as you like

xxxxxxxxxxxxxxxxxxxxxxxxxxxxxxxxxxxxxxxxxxx

Procedure:

1. Take an electric pressure cooker, select the sauté in 6-qt and adjust it on medium heat.

2. Add the oil. When the oil becomes hot, stir and cook the onion and sausages until it gets lightly browned.

3. Add the garlic and cook it for 1 minute.

4. Stir and cook the chicken broth in 4 cups, salt, pepper, and rice.

5. Lock up the lid, close the pressure–release valve.

6. Adjust it to low heat for 3 minutes.

7. Let it release naturally for 10 minutes.

8. Quick the release of any remaining pressure.

9. Ricer gets tender.

10. Select the sauté setting, adjust it on the low heat.

11. Stir and cook in the remaining broth and chicken.

12. Cook it until the chicken gets heated through, for 5 minutes.

13. Sprinkle it with green onion if you want.

14. Serve it with hot sauce and enjoy your meal.

Recipe 4 - Cooker Fabulous Fajitas

This amazing fajitas recipe makes your meal more desirable. Its taste becomes more incredible if you serve it with healthy and colorful vegetables.

Total Prep Time: 25 min

Yield: 8

List of Ingredients:

- Beefsteak top sirloin 1½ lbs. (cut into thin strips)
- Ground cumin 1½ tsp.
- Seasons salt 1/2 tsp.
- Chili powder 1/2 tsp.
- Red pepper flakes crushed 1/4 to 1/2 tsp.
- Canola oil 2 tbsp.
- Lemon juice 2 tbsp.
- Minced garlic cloves 1
- Water 1/2 cup
- Thinly sliced sweet red pepper 1 large
- Thinly sliced onion 1 large
- Flour tortillas 8 (8 inches) warm

Optional: jalapeno pepper, avocado sliced, chopped tomatoes, and cheddar shredded cheese

xxxxxxxxxxxxxxxxxxxxxxxxxxxxxxxxxxxxxxxxxxxxx

Procedure:

1. Take a bowl, toss the steak with the cumin, chili powder, salt, and red pepper flakes.

2. Select the sauté setting in 6-qt on an electric pressure cooker.

3. Adjust it on medium heat, add the oil; when the oil becomes hot, brown the meat in batches and then remove.

4. Add lemon juice, water, and garlic to the cooker and stir it to loosen any brown bits.

5. Now press the cancel, return the beef to the cooker.

6. Lock up the lid, close the pressure–release valve.

7. Adjust it to high heat for 20 minutes.

8. Let it release naturally for 10 minutes.

9. Quick the release of any remaining pressure.

10. Take a slotted spoon and remove the steaks and keep it warm.

11. After this, add the red pepper and onion to the cooker.

12. Look at the lid and close pressure – release valve.

13. Serve the vegetables and tortilla with steak and desired to top.

14. Serve it immediately and enjoy it.

Recipe 5 - Hearty Pork & Black Beans Nachos

These incredible hearty pork & black beans nachos make your dinner more surprising; this nacho platter is a quick dish and takes less effort. Try this one and enjoy it.

Total Prep Time: 40 min

Yield: 10

List of Ingredients:

- Beef jerky 1 package (4 ounces)
- Spareribs pork 3 lbs. (cut into 2 rib section)
- Rinsed and drained black beans 4 cans (15 ounces each)
- Chopped onion 1 cup
- Bacon strips 6 (cooked and crumbled)
- Minced garlic 4 tsp.
- Red pepper flakes crushed 1 tsp.
- Beef broth 4 cups (divided)
- Tortillas chips
- Topping optional: cheddar shredded cheese, sour cream, jalapeno pickle slices, thinly sliced green onion, and chopped tomatoes.

xxxxxxxxxxxxxxxxxxxxxxxxxxxxxxxxxxxxxxxxxx

Procedure:

1. Take a food processor, add pulse beef jerky until it gets finely ground.

2. Working in the batches, add 1½ lbs. of rib in a 6 –qt in an electric pressure cooker.

3. Top it with half of the jerky, 2 cans of beans, 1/2 cup of onion, 2 cups of broth, 2 tsp. garlic, and ½ tsp. of red pepper flakes.

4. Lock up the lid, close the pressure–release valve.

5. Adjust it to high heat for 40 minutes.

6. Let it release naturally for 10 minutes.

7. Quick the release of any remaining pressure.

8. Remove this pork from the pressure cooker.

9. Now make the second batch with the same ingredients and repeat the same procedure.

10. When it cools enough to deal, remove all the meats from the bones, discard the bones.

11. Shred the meat with the help of two forks.

12. Now return to the pressure cooker and make a sauté setting and adjust it for high heat. Strain the mixture of pork.

13. Discard the juice, serve it with the chips, and do topping of it as you want.

14. Serve it warm and enjoy it.

Recipe 6 - Pressure Cooker Sauerbraten

This recipe of the pressure cooker makes a meal quickly and it takes less time to get ready. Make it with beef and vegetables, so let's try it for your family.

Total Prep Time: 20 min

Yield: 4

List of Ingredients:

- Whole cloves 4
- Peppercorn 4
- Bay leaf 1
- Water 1/2 cup
- White vinegar 1/2 cup
- Sugar 2 tsp.
- Salt 1/2 tsp.
- Dash ground ginger
- Top round steak boneless beef 1 pound (cut into ½ inch cube)
- carrots 3 medium (cut into 1/2 inch slice)
- celery ribs 2 (cut into 1/2 inch slice)
- chopped onion 1 small
- crushed gingersnaps 1/3 cup
- cooked hot egg noodles
- fresh chopped parsley ground coarsely pepper

xxxxxxxxxxxxxxxxxxxxxxxxxxxxxxxxxxxxxxxxxxx

Procedure:

1. Take a double thickness of cheesecloth, place the peppercorn, bay leaves, and cloves, bring up the corners of the cloth and tie it up with the kitchen strings to form it like a bag.

2. Take a large bowl, put the vinegar, salt water, ginger, and sugar; now add the beef and spices bag and wait for room temperature for 30 minutes.

3. Take an electric pressure cooker of 6-qt. And add celery, onion, and carrots.

4. Look up the cooker lid and close the pressure–release valve.

5. Adjust the pressure on high heat for about 10 minutes.

6. Release quick pressure.

7. Adjust for medium heat and select the sauté setting and bring it to boil.

8. Discard the spices bag and stir it into the gingersnaps.

9. Stir and cook until it gets thickened for 3 minutes.

10. Serve it with egg noodles.

11. Top it with parsley leaves and pepper.

12. Serve it warm and enjoy it.

Recipe 7 - Red Calm Sauce

This recipe will make your day. Its taste is impressive, and its classy combination of pasta and red sauce makes your meal more incredible.

Total Prep Time: 25 min

Yield: 4

List of Ingredients:

- Canola oil 1 tbsp.
- Chopped onion 1 medium
- Minced garlic cloves 2
- Chopped clams, undrained 2 cans of 6½ ounces
- Diced tomatoes undrained 1 can of 14½ ounces
- Tomato paste 1 can of 6 ounces
- Fresh minced parsley ¼ cup
- Bay leaf 1
- Sugar 1 tsp.
- Dried basil 1 tsp.
- Dried thyme 1/2 tsp.
- Cooked and drained linguine 6 ounces

xxxxxxxxxxxxxxxxxxxxxxxxxxxxxxxxxxxxxxxxx

Procedure:

1. Take an electric pressure cooker, select the sauté in 6-qt and adjust it on medium heat.

2. Now add the oil, when the oil becomes hot, add the onion sauté until it gets tender, add garlic and cook it for 1 minute. Press the cancel.

3. Stir in the 1 to 8 ingredients, Lock the lid in place and cook it on high for 3 minutes more.

4. Allow it naturally to release the pressure for 5 minutes and then quickly release any remaining pressure.

5. Discard all the bay leaf, serve it with linguine.

6. Serve it immediately and enjoy.

Recipe 8 - Chicken with Olives and Artichokes

This chicken recipe with olives and artichokes makes an incredible taste, and it serves as a main course dish. Enjoy it. What are you waiting for?

Total Prep Time: 30 min

Yield: 8

List of Ingredients:

- All-purpose flour 1/4 cup
- Garlic salt 1/2 tsp.
- Pepper 1/4 tsp.
- Chicken thigh bone- in 8 (3 lbs.) if desired skin remove
- Olive oil 1 tbsp.
- Thinly sliced garlic cloves 4
- Zest grated lemon 1 tbsp.
- Dried thyme 1/2 tsp.
- Dried crushed rosemary 1/2 tsp.
- Quarter water-packed artichoke hearts 1 can (14 ounces)
- Pimento stuffed olives 1/2 cup
- Bay leaf 1
- Orange juice 1½ cup
- Chicken both 3/4 cup
- Honey 2 tbsp.

xxxxxxxxxxxxxxxxxxxxxxxxxxxxxxxxxxxxxxxxxxx

Procedure:

1. Take a shallow bowl, mix the garlic salt, flour, and pepper.

2. Take the chicken thighs, dip it into the flour mixture, coat it from both sides, and shake off its excess.

3. Take an electric pressure cooker, sauté it on the setting on a 6-qt on medium heat, add the oil, put the chicken thighs, and get browned from all the sides.

4. Now sprinkle it with lemon zest, garlic, rosemary, and thyme on the chicken.

5. Top it with the artichokes heart, bay leaves, and olive.

6. Take a bowl, mix up the broth, honey, and orange juice; put it on the top, lock the lid, close the pressure, and release the valve.

7. Adjust it on high heat for 15 minutes and allow this pressure to release by self for 10 minutes.

8. Then do the quick release of the remaining pressure.

9. Remove all the bay leaves.

10. Mix up the gremolata ingredients in the small bowl, sprinkle it over the artichokes mixture and chicken.

11. Serve it warm and enjoy your dish.

Recipe 9 - Pork Pozole

This recipe will make your dish lightly spiced, but its taste becomes more delicious and unique. Let's try it today and enjoy it.

Total Prep Time: 25 min

Yield: 6

List of Ingredients:

- Undrained diced tomatoes 1 can (14½ ounces)
- Green chilies with mild diced tomatoes 1 can (14½ ounces)
- Green enchilada sauce 1 can of 10 ounces
- Finely chopped onion 1 medium
- Minced garlic cloves 3
- Ground cumin 2 tsp.
- Salt 1/4 tsp.
- Country style boneless pork ribs 1 pound
- Drained and rinsed hominy 1 can of 15½ ounces
- Finely chopped carrot 2 medium
- Fresh minced cilantro, lime wedge
- Corn tortillas 6 inches, optional

xxxxxxxxxxxxxxxxxxxxxxxxxxxxxxxxxxxxxxxxxxx

Procedure:

1. Take an electric pressure cooker in a 6-qt, now add and combine the 1 to 7 ingredients add pork.

2. Lock the lid and make sure the vent is closed.

3. Now select the manual setting and adjust it to high heat for 20 minutes.

4. When finished cooking, allow the pressure cooker to release naturally according to the manufacturer's direction.

5. Add the hominy and carrots.

6. Lock the lid in place and cook it for 5 minutes more.

7. Allow it naturally to release the pressure for 10 minutes and then quickly release any remaining pressure.

8. Remove this pork from the pressure cooker, cut it into bite-sized pieces, return it to the pressure cooker.

9. Serve it with lime wedges and cilantro.

10. If you want, then add corn tortillas.

11. Serve it immediately and enjoy it.

Recipe 10 - Carolina Shrimp & Cheddar Grits

This Carolina shrimp & cheddar grits recipe makes healthy food; your homies will love it if you serve it with cheddar cheese.

Total Prep Time: 20

Yield: 6

List of Ingredients:

- Water 4 cup
- Minced garlic cloves 1 large
- Salt 1/2 tsp.
- Pepper 1/4 tsp.
- Old-fashioned grits uncooked 1 cup
- Cheddar shredded cheese 2 cups
- Cubed butter 1/4 cup
- Cook shrimps peeled and deveined 1 pound (31-40 per pound)
- Seeded and finely chopped tomatoes 2 medium
- Green onion finely chopped 4
- Fresh minced parsley 2 tbsp.
- Lemon juice 4 tsp.
- Cajun seasoning 2 – 3 tsp.

xxxxxxxxxxxxxxxxxxxxxxxxxxxxxxxxxxxxxxxxxxx

Procedure:

1. Take an electric pressure cooker, sauté setting will be on a 6-qt and adjust it on high heat.

2. Add the 1 to 4 ingredients, stir them to combine, and bring it to a boil.

3. Now slowly add the grits, stirring, and constantly avoid adding lumps.

4. Select the sauté setting, now slow down the heat and cook for 15 minutes.

5. Stir it on cheese and in the butter until it gets melted.

6. Stir it in the remaining ingredients.

7. Cook it for 3 to 4 minutes or until it gets heated through.

8. Serve it immediately and enjoy it.

Recipe 11 - Brussels Sprouts

This recipe will take minimal effort, but it makes a fantastic dish. It seems more delicious when it is served with nuts and vegetables.

Total Prep Time: 25 min

Yield: 10

List of Ingredients:

- Fresh and sliced Brussels Sprouts 2 lb.
- Chopped large apples 2
- Cranberries, dried 3 cups
- Crumbled and cooked bacon strips 8
- Syrup of Maple 1 by 4 cup
- Olive oil 2 tbsp.
- Ground Coarsely pepper 1/2 tsp.
- Salt 1 tsp.
- Toasted pecans or hazelnuts chopped 3/4 cup
- Vinegar of Cider 1/3 cup

xxxxxxxxxxxxxxxxxxxxxxxxxxxxxxxxxxxxxxxxxxxx

Procedure:

1. Add and mix the Brussels sprouts, cranberries, apples, and half of the bacon crumbled.

2. Take a slight bowl, combine the syrup, oil, vinegar, pepper, and salt.

3. Pour it over the mixture of Brussels sprouts, and toss it coat.

4. Convert it into 6 qt size. in an electric pressure cooker.

5. Lock the lid and make sure the vent is closed.

6. Now select the manual setting and adjust it to high heat for just 3 minutes.

7. When it becomes finished cooking, allow the pressure cooker to release naturally.

8. Now sprinkle the hazelnuts also with the remaining bacon.

9. Serve it immediately and enjoy it.

Recipe 12 - Cooker Boeuf Bourguignon

This recipe has an amazing taste with the boeuf bourguignon in a pressure cooker. Make it today for a family feast and have fun.

Total Prep Time: 35 min

Yield: 6

List of Ingredients:

- Stew meat beef 3 lbs.
- Red dry wine 1¾ cup
- Olive oil 3 tbsp.
- Dried minced onion 3 tbsp.
- Dried parsley flakes 2 tbsp.
- Bay leaf 1
- Dried thyme 1 tsp.
- Pepper 1/4 tsp.
- Chopped bacon strips 8
- Fresh whole mushrooms 1 pound
- Peeled pearl onion 24 (about 2 cups)
- Minced garlic cloves 2
- All-purpose flour 1/3 cup
- Salt 1 tsp.
- Cooked hot whole wheat egg noodles (optional)

xxxxxxxxxxxxxxxxxxxxxxxxxxxxxxxxxxxxxxxxxxx

Procedure:

1. Take a large shallow dish, add the beef, oil, wine, and seasoning.

2. Coat the beef and keep it in the refrigerator overnight.

3. For an electric pressure cooker, select the sauté setting on 6-qt and adjust it on medium heat.

4. Add the bacon, cook until it gets crisp.

5. Remove it from the slotted spoon; drain it on the paper towel.

6. Reserve the 1 tbsp. from the discarding drippings in the pressure cooker.

7. Add onion and mushrooms for dripping, stir and cook it until it gets tender.

8. Add the garlic and cook it for 1 minute or longer. Press the cancel.

9. Drain the beef and reserve the marinade. Add the beef to the pressure cooker.

10. Sprinkle the beef, salt and flour toss it to coat.

11. Top it with bacon and reserved the marinade.

12. Lock up the lid, close the pressure–release valve.

13. Adjust it to high heat for 20 minutes.

14. Let it release naturally for 10 minutes.

15. Quick the release of any remaining pressure.

16. Select the sauté setting, adjust it on low heat.

17. Uncovered and simmer until sauces reach the desired thickness for 15 to 20 minutes.

18. Remove the bay leaf.

19. If you want, serve the stew with noodles.

20. Serve it warm and enjoy it.

Recipe 13 - Chinese Ribs

This recipe is a delicious recipe made at dinner. It takes less time to get ready, and Ribs are easy to make and seem appetizing as let's enjoy.

Total Prep Time: 30 min

Yield: 6

List of Ingredients:

- Pork ribs country-style boneless 3 lbs.
- Green onion 6 cut Int no 1 inch
- Sliced water chestnuts 1 can drained 8 ounces
- Hoisin sauce 3 by 4 cup
- Water 1 by 2 cup
- Soy sauce 3 tbsp.
- Chicken stock or Sherry 2 tbsp.
- Minced garlic cloves 5
- Minced fresh ginger root 1 tbsp.
- Corn syrup 1 tbsp.
- Marmalade of Orange 1 tbsp.
- Pie spice pumpkin 1 tsp.
- Red crushed pepper flakes 2 tsp.
- Cornstarch 1 - 2 tbsp.
- Cooked hot rice on your choice
- Green onion thinly sliced optional

xxxxxxxxxxxxxxxxxxxxxxxxxxxxxxxxxxxxxxxxxx

Procedure:

1. Take an electric pressure cooker, place the pork, water and green onion, chestnut in 6qt.

2. Mix sherry, soy sauce, water, hoisin sauce, gingerroot, garlic, marmalade, corn syrup, pepper flakes, and pie spice in bowl.

3. Pour it over the pork, Lock the lid and make sure the vent is closed.

4. Now select the manual setting and adjust it to high heat for just 25 minutes.

5. When it becomes finished cooking, allow the pressure cooker to release naturally for 10 minutes.

6. Remove the pork to the serving plate and keep it warm.

7. Skim the fat from the cooking juice.

8. Select the sauté adjust and set it on medium heat and bring it to boil.

9. Take a minor bowl and mix the water and cornstarch until it gets smooth.

10. Stir the mixture of cornstarch in a pressure stove gradually.

11. Being it boil, stir and cook it until it gets thickened for 2 minutes.

12. Serve the ribs with the sauce.

13. If you want, add rice and green onion.

14. Serve it warm and enjoy it.

Recipe 14 - Sausage & Waffle Bake

This sausage & waffle bake recipe makes interesting and represented in the breakfast. It is pretty delicious and an easy dish, so let's give it a try today.

Total Prep Time: 20 min

Yield: 6

List of Ingredients:

- Spicy bulk breakfast pork sausage 1 pound
- Rubbed sage 1½ tsp.
- Fennel seed 1/4 tsp.
- Bite-sized pieces frozen waffles 5
- Eggs large 4
- Half and half cream 2/3 cup
- Maple syrup 2 tbsp.
- Salt 1/8 tsp.
- Pepper 1/8 tsp.
- Cheddar shredded cheese 1 cup

xxxxxxxxxxxxxxxxxxxxxxxxxxxxxxxxxxxxxxxxxx

Procedure:

1. Take an electric pressure cooker adjust it in medium heat now select a sauté or setting on 6-qt.

2. Cook the sausages until it gets to change their color for 6 – 8 minutes.

3. Makes its crumbles, drain it, and add fennel and sage.

4. Now press cancel places these waffles in a greased 1-1/2 qt, baking dish top it with the mixture of sausages.

5. Take a bowl, mix the cream, eggs, seasoning, and syrup.

6. Pour it over the sausages and waffles.

7. Top it with the cheese.

8. Cover the baking dish with foil.

9. Clean up the pressure cooker.

10. Place the trivet insert and add 1 cup of water to the pressure cooker.

11. Make a sling-like, fold it an 18x12 in a piece of the foil into lengthwise into third.

12. Use these slings, to lower the dish onto the divert insert.

13. Lock up the lid, close the pressure–release valve.

14. Adjust it to high heat for 20 minutes.

15. Let it release naturally for 5 minutes.

16. Quick the release of any remaining pressure.

17. Using the foil sling, remove carefully from the baking dish.

18. Serve it with the maple syrup.

Recipe 15 - Risotto with Shrimp and Asparagus

This one is a quick method of making risotto every time; if you want to go somewhere, you can make it and enjoy it with your homies.

Total Prep Time: 35 min

Yield: 8

List of Ingredients:

- Olive oil 2 tbsp.
- Minced garlic cloves 9
- Peeled and deveined uncooked shrimp 2 lbs. (26-30 per pound)
- Unsalted butter 4 tbsp.
- Italian salad 1/2 cup
- Trimmed fresh asparagus 1 pound
- Diced finely onion 1 small
- Uncooked arborio rice 1-2/3 cups
- White wine 1 cup
- chicken broth reduced sodium 4 cups
- Parmesan shredded cheese 1/2 cup
- Pepper and salt to taste

xxxxxxxxxxxxxxxxxxxxxxxxxxxxxxxxxxxxxxxxxxxx

Procedure:

1. Take an electric pressure cooker, select the sauté in 6-qt and adjust it on medium heat.

2. Now add the oil; when the oil becomes hot, add 3 minced cloves of garlic and cook it for 1 minute.

3. Add the shrimp, cook, and stir it until the shrimp change its color, for 5 minutes.

4. Add 1 tbsp. of butter and Italian salad for dressing, stir it until the butter melts.

5. Add asparagus, cook it until it gets tender for 3-5 minutes.

6. Remove it and keep it warm.

7. Take the remaining 3 tbsp. of butter to get warm until it gets melted.

8. Add diced onion and cook it until it gets tender for 4-5 minutes.

9. Now add the remaining 6 minced garlic cloves and cook it for 1 minute.

10. Add the rice and stir and cook it for 2 minutes.

11. Stir in 1/2 cup of wine, stir and cook it until absorbed.

12. Add the remaining 1/2 wine and broth and also 1/4 cup of cheese.

13. Now press the cancel.

14. Lock the lid and make sure the vent is closed.

15. Now select the manual setting and adjust it to high heat for 8 minutes.

16. When it becomes finished cooking, allow the pressure cooker to release naturally.

17. Serve the shrimp mixture on risotto.

18. Season it with salt and pepper.

19. Sprinkle it with the remaining 1/4 cup of cheese.

20. Serve it warm and enjoy it.

Recipe 16 - Sweet 'n' Sour Pork

This recipe and its ingredients seems the oldest recipe dish, but its taste and texture becomes the same as delicious, enjoy it

Total Prep Time: 15 min

Yield: 6

List of Ingredients:

- Paprika 2 tbsp. plus 1½ tsp.
- Loin roast boneless pork 1½ lbs. (cut into 1-inch strips)
- Canola oil 1 tbsp.
- Pineapple unsweetened chunks 1 can (20 ounces)
- Chopped onion 1 medium
- Chopped green pepper 1 medium
- Cider vinegar 1/4 cup
- Packed brown sugar 3 tbsp.
- Soy sauce reduced-sodium 3 tbsp.
- Worcestershire sauce 1 tbsp.
- Salt ½ tsp.
- Cornstarch 2 tbsp.
- Coldwater 1/4 cup
- Chopped green onion, thinly sliced
- Hot cooked rice, optional

xxxxxxxxxxxxxxxxxxxxxxxxxxxxxxxxxxxxxxxxxx

Procedure:

1. Take a large shallow dish, add the pork, a few pieces at a time, and turn to coat.

2. Take an electric pressure cooker and adjust it on medium heat, now select sauté setting on 6-qt in.

3. Add oil and brown these pork in batches.

4. Return all the pork to the pressure cooker.

5. Drain this pineapple, reserving the juice, and refrigerate the pineapple.

6. Add the pineapple juice, green pepper, onion, brown sugar, soy sauce, vinegar, Worcestershire sauce, and salt to the pressure cooker.

7. Lock up the lid, close the pressure–release valve.

8. Adjust it to high heat for 10 minutes.

9. Let it release naturally.

10. Quick the release of any remaining pressure.

11. Select the sauté setting, and adjust it on high heat, and bring it to boil it.

12. Take a small bowl, mix the cornstarch and the water until it gets smooth.

13. Stir into the pork mixture gradually.

14. Add the pineapple, cook, and stir it until sauce becomes thickened for 1-2 minutes.

15. If you want, serve it with rice and sprinkle it with green onion.

16. Serve it warm and enjoy your meal.

Recipe 17 - Tuna Noodles Casserole

Want to go for easy? We have a solution to make the dishes in a pressure cooker, make it, and enjoy its taste and texture superbly delicious with this recipe.

Total Prep Time: 15 min

Yield: 10

List of Ingredients:

- Cubed butter 1/4 cup
- Fresh sliced mushrooms 1/2 lbs.
- Chopped onion 1 medium
- Chopped sweet pepper 1 medium
- Salt 1 tsp.
- Pepper 1 tsp.
- Minced garlic cloves 2
- All-purpose flour 1/4 cup
- Chicken broth sodium-reduced 2 cups
- Half and half cream 2 cups
- Uncooked egg noodles 4 cups (8 ounces)
- Light tuna in water 3 cans (5 ounces each)
- Lemon juice 2 tbsp.
- Monterey shredded jack cheese 2 cups
- Frozen peas 2 cups
- Crushed potato chips 2 cups

xxxxxxxxxxxxxxxxxxxxxxxxxxxxxxxxxxxxxxxxxxx

Procedure:

1. Take an electric pressure cooker, select the sauté in 6-qt and adjust it on medium heat.

2. Add butter; when it gets melted, add the mushrooms, sweet pepper, onions, salt 1/2 tsp., pepper 1/2 tsp..

1. Stir and cook it until it gets tender for 6 – 8 minutes.

2. Add the garlic cook it for 1 minute longer.

3. Stir in the flour until it gets blended.

4. Whisk the broth gradually until it gets to boil.

5. Cooked and stir it until it gets thickened for 1-2 minutes.

6. Stir in the cream and the noodles.

7. Lock the lid and make sure the vent is closed.

8. Now select the manual setting and adjust it to high heat for 3 minutes.

9. When it becomes finished cooking, allow the pressure cooker to release the naturally for 3 minutes.

10. After this, take a small bowl, combine the tuna, remaining salt and pepper, and lemon juice.

11. Select the sauté setting on low heat.

12. Stir in the cheese, tuna mixture, and the peas in the noodles mixture.

13. Cook until it gets heated through.

14. Before serving, sprinkle the potato chips

15. Serve it immediately and enjoy it.

Recipe 18 - Mustard Pork Roast

This recipe has an amazing texture and super delicious. Serve it with delightful mustard sauce, try it today and have fun.

Total Prep Time: 90 min

Yield: 8

List of Ingredients:

- Shoulder bitt roast boneless pork 1 (3-4 lbs.)
- Salt 3/4 tsp.
- Canola oil 1 tbsp.
- Pepper 1/4 tbsp.
- Drained diced tomatoes 1 can (14½ ounces)
- Chopped onion 1 medium
- Dry red wine 1/2 cup
- Beef broth 1 can (14½ ounces)
- Minced garlic cloves 6
- Honey 2 tbsp.
- Molasses 2 tbsp.
- Dried thyme 1 tsp.
- Cornstarch 2 tbsp.
- Stoneground mustard 3/4 cup
- Coldwater 2 tbsp.

xxxxxxxxxxxxxxxxxxxxxxxxxxxxxxxxxxxxxxxxxxx

Procedure:

1. Take an electric pressure cooker, select the sauté and adjust it to high heat in a 6-qt.

2. Sprinkle the roast with pepper and salt, heat the oil brown the roast from all the sides.

3. Add tomatoes and the onion, pour out the broth, and also wine around the meat.

4. Combine the garlic, mustard, molasses, honey, and thyme on the pork.

5. Lock up the lid, close the pressure–release valve

6. Adjust it to high heat and set the time to 90 minutes.

7. Let it release naturally for 10 minutes after the finished cooking.

8. Quick the release of any remaining pressure according to the instruction.

9. Remove the roast, and let it stand for 15 minutes.

10. After this, skim the fat from the cooking juice.

11. Select the sauté and adjust it on high heat and let the juice to get a boil.

12. Take a small bowl, mix the cornstarch and water until it gets smooth, and gradually stir it into the cooking juice.

13. Stir and cook it until the sauce gets thickened for 1-2 minutes.

14. Shred and slice of pork and serve it with sauce.

15. Serve it at once and enjoy your roast.

Recipe 19 - Denver Omelet Frittata

The omelet has an incredible taste when serving ham, onion, and pepper. Make and serve it in your breakfast or serve it to your friends as a special breakfast treat.

Total Prep Time: 35 min

Yield: 6

List of Ingredients:

- Potato Tukon Gold sliced and peeled 1 medium
- Olive oil 1 tbsp.
- Thinly sliced onion 1 small
- Water 1 cup
- Eggs 12 large
- pepper sauce Hot 1 tsp.
- Salt 1/2 tsp.
- Pepper 1/4 tsp.
- Sliced and chopped deli ham 8 ounces
- Chopped green pepper 1/2 cup
- Cheddar shredded cheese 1 cup

xxxxxxxxxxxxxxxxxxxxxxxxxxxxxxxxxxxxxxxxxxxxx

Procedure:

1. Take an electric pressure cooker, select the sauté in 6-qt and adjust it on high heat.

2. Heat the oil, add onion and potatoes, cook, and then stir it for about 4 to 6 minutes until the potatoes get lightly browned.

3. Convert it into a round greased 6 to 7 in a baking dish (1½ qt)

4. Clean up the pressure cooker and pour the water into it.

5. Take a big bowl, whisk the eggs, salt, pepper, pepper sauce, stir in the green pepper and ham, and the ½ cup of cheese.

6. Top it with the remaining cheese.

7. Cover this baking sheet with the foil and place it on the trivet with the handles. Lower it into the pressure cooker.

8. Lock the lid and make sure the vent is closed.

9. Now select the manual setting, adjust it to high heat, and set it for 35 minutes.

10. When it becomes finished cooking, allow the pressure cooker to release the naturally for 10 minutes.

11. According to manufacturers' instructions, quick release any of the remaining pressure.

12. Serve it warm and immediately and enjoy it.

Recipe 20 - Cooker Cranberry Apple Grains

This recipe is made with the perfect grain together, and its taste becomes more delightful and delicious. It's a healthy recipe you can serve in breakfast.

Total Prep Time: 25 min

Yield: 10

List of Ingredients:

- Sugar 1 cup
- Medium apples 2 (chopped and peeled)
- Wheat berries 1/2 cup
- Fresh cranberries 1 cup
- Rinsed quinoa 1/2 cup
- Pearl barley medium 1/2 cup
- Walnut 1/2 cup (chopped)
- Brown packed sugar 1/2 cup
- Ground cinnamon 1½ to 2 tsp.
- Water 6 cup
- Oat bran 1/2 cup
- Brown sugar, milk, chopped walnut, or apple pieces (optional)

xxxxxxxxxxxxxxxxxxxxxxxxxxxxxxxxxxxxxxxxxxx

Procedure:

1. Take an electric pressure cooker in a 6-qt.

2. Combine the 1 to 11 ingredients.

3. Lock up the lid, close the pressure–release valve.

4. Adjust it to high heat for 25 minutes.

5. Let it release naturally.

6. Quick the release of any remaining pressure.

7. Serve it with the remaining optional ingredients.

Recipe 21 - Buffalo Shrimp Mac & Cheese

This recipe is full of rich in cream and spicy too. It's a new way to serve and beat this crowd-pleasing dish. You must try this recipe.

Total Prep Time: 15 min

Yield: 6

List of Ingredients:

- Milk 2 cup
- Half and half cream 1 cup
- Unsalted butter 1 tbsp.
- Ground mustard 1 tsp.
- Onion powder 1/2 tsp.
- White pepper 1/4 tsp.
- Ground nutmeg 1/4 tsp.
- Uncooked elbow macaroni 1½ cup
- Cheddar shredded cheese 2 cups
- Swiss and Gouda shredded cheese 1 cup
- Cooked frozen salad shrimps, thawed 3/4 pound
- Blue crumble cheese 1 cup
- Louisiana style hot sauce 2 tbsp.
- Fresh minced chives 2 tbsp.
- Fresh minced parsley 2 tbsp.
- Louisiana style hot sauce (optional additional)

xxxxxxxxxxxxxxxxxxxxxxxxxxxxxxxxxxxxxxxxx

Procedure:

1. Take an electric pressure cooker in 6 qt size, add and combine the 1 to 7 ingredients, stir it in macaroni.

2. Lock up the lid, close the pressure–release valve.

3. Adjust it to high heat for 3 minutes.

4. Let it release naturally for 4 minutes.

5. Quick the release of any remaining pressure according to the direction of the manufacturer.

6. Now select the sauté setting and adjust it to medium heat.

7. Stir in the shredded cheese, blue cheese, shrimps, and hot sauce.

8. Cook it for 5-6 minutes until heated through.

9. Stir it in the chives and parsley before serving.

10. If you want, then add the hot sauce.

11. Serve it warm and immediately and enjoy it.

Recipe 22 - Cooker Turkey with Berry Compote

This yummy and incredible recipe makes everyone happy because its turkey flavor dish and its combination with the berries make the perfect sauce, let's try it today and enjoy it.

Total Prep Time: 45 min

Yield: 12

List of Ingredients:

- Salt 1 tsp.
- Garlic powder 1/2 tsp.
- Dried thyme 1/2 tsp.
- Pepper 1/2 tsp.
- Skinless, boneless turkey breast halves (2 lbs. each)
- Water 1/3 cup
- For Compote:
- Peeled and finely chopped apple 2 medium
- Fresh raspberries 2 cups
- Fresh blueberries 2 cups
- White grape juice 1 cup
- Crushed red pepper flakes ¼ tsp.
- Ground ginger ¼ tsp.

xxxxxxxxxxxxxxxxxxxxxxxxxxxxxxxxxxxxxxxxxxxxx

Procedure:

1. Take an electric pressure cooker, place in 6-qt in, and add garlic, salt, pepper, and thyme and rub it on the turkey breast.

2. Pour the water around the turkey.

3. Lock up the lid, close the pressure–release valve.

4. Adjust it to high heat for 30 minutes.

5. Let it release naturally for 10 minutes.

6. Quick the release of any remaining pressure.

7. Adjust the thermometer in the turkey breast it should be read at 165°F.

8. Remove the turkey and the juice from the pressure cooker.

9. Tent it with foil and let it stand before making the slicing.

10. Adjust the sauté setting and put it on low heat.

11. Add all the compote ingredients uncovered, and simmer until the mixture becomes slightly thickened and apples become tender for 15 to 20 minutes.

12. Stir it occasionally and serve the turkey with the compote.

13. Serve it warm and enjoy it.

Recipe 23 - Apple Pear Compote

This recipe has the combination of apple with pears, and its taste is delicious and full of nutrition, and you can serve it warm for breakfast. Let's try it now and have a nice pear compote this evening.

Total Prep Time: 30 minutes

Yield: 8 cups

List of Ingredients:

- Chopped pear 3 (medium)
- Peeled and chopped apples 5 (medium)
- Packed brown sugar 1/2 cup
- Thinly sliced orange 1 medium
- Lemon juice 2 tbsp.
- Butter cubed 1/3 cup
- Maple syrup 1/2 cup
- Ground cinnamon 2 tsp.
- Ginger ground 1 tsp.
- Orange juice 5 tbsp.
- Cornstarch 4 tsp.
- Dried cranberries 1/2 cup
- Toasted pecans, chopped (optional)
- Whipped cream (optional)

xxxxxxxxxxxxxxxxxxxxxxxxxxxxxxxxxxxxxxxxxx

Procedure:

1. Take an electric pressure cooker in 6 qt size, combine the 1 to 10 ingredients.

2. Stir the orange juice 2 tbsp..

3. Lock up the lid, close the pressure–release valve.

4. Adjust it to high heat on a manual setting and set the time for 6 minutes.

5. Let it release naturally for 5 minutes.

6. Quick the release of any remaining pressure according to the direction of the manufacturer.

7. Now select the sauté setting and adjust it to high heat, cook it until the liquid gets to boil.

8. Take a small bowl, mix up the cornstarch, orange juice until it gets smooth.

9. Stir it gradually in the fruit mixture.

10. Stir and cook it until the sauce gets thickened for 1-2 minutes.

11. If you want, then top it with whipped cream and also with pecans.

12. Serve it immediately and enjoy your meal.

Recipe 24 - Cooker Mediterranean Chicken Orzo

This recipe of Mediterranean chicken orzo has an amazing taste and its combination with the herbs and olives bright flavor make your dish impressive, so let's try it today.

Total Prep Time: 20 min

Yield: 6

List of Ingredients:

- Chicken thighs skinless boneless 6 (1½ lbs.) cut into 1-inch slice
- Chicken broth reduced sodium 2 cups
- Chopped tomatoes 2 medium
- Pitted sliced green olives 1 cup, drained
- Pitted sliced ripe olives 1 cup drained
- Chopped and halved lengthwise, carrot 1 large
- Chopped finely red onion 1 small
- Grated lemon zest 1 tbsp.
- Lemon juice 3 tbsp.
- Butter 2 tbsp.
- Herbs de Provence 1 tbsp.
- Uncooked orzo pasta 1 cup

xxxxxxxxxxxxxxxxxxxxxxxxxxxxxxxxxxxxxxxxxxxxx

Procedure:

1. Take an electric pressure cooker, in 6-qt in, add and combine the 1 to 11 ingredients.

2. Lock up the lid, close the pressure–release valve.

3. Adjust it to high heat for 8 minutes.

4. Let it release naturally.

5. Quick the release of any remaining pressure.

6. Add the orzo, lock up the lid, close the pressure–release valve.

7. Adjust it to low heat for 3 minutes.

8. Let it release naturally for 4 minutes.

9. Quick the release of any remaining pressure.

10. Before serving, let it stand for 8-10 minutes.

11. Serve it warm and enjoy your meal.

Recipe 25 - Cherry & Spice Rice Pudding

This recipe is served as a lovely meal; it is an easier and quick meal. Make it and enjoy it. Let's try it and serve this tasty pudding with your favorite cherries.

Total Prep Time: 20 min

Yield: 12

List of Ingredients:

- Cooked rice 4 cup
- Evaporated milk 1 can (12 ounces)
- Milk 1 cup
- Sugar 1/3 cup
- Water 1/4 cup
- Dried cherries 3/4 cup
- Butter softened 3 tbsp.
- Vanilla extract 2 tsp.
- Ground cinnamon 1/2 tsp.
- Nutmeg ground 1/4 tsp.

xxxxxxxxxxxxxxxxxxxxxxxxxxxxxxxxxxxxxxxxxxxx

Procedure:

1. Take an electric pressure cooker grease it generously in 6 qt size.

2. Add the milk, rice, sugar, and also water; stir, and combine them.

3. Stir in the remaining ingredients.

4. Lock up the lid, close the pressure–release valve.

5. Adjust it to high heat for 20 minutes.

6. Let it release naturally for 10 minutes.

7. Quick the release of any remaining pressure.

8. Serve it cold or warm it's up to you.

9. Refrigerate the leftover pudding.

10. Serve it and enjoy this pudding.

Recipe 26 - Cooker Pork Chili Verde

This recipe stews it with the onion and jalapenos, and the green enchilada sauce makes your meal healthier and more delicious, serve it with warm tortillas and with cream so enjoy it.

Total Prep Time: 30

Yield: 8

List of Ingredients:

- Canola oil 3 tbsp.
- Sirloin roast boneless pork 1 (3 lbs.) cut in cubes 1 inch
- Carrot sliced 4 medium
- Thinly sliced onion 1 medium
- Minced garlic cloves 4
- Green enchilada sauce 1 can of 28 ounces
- Seeded and chopped jalapeno pepper 2
- Fresh minced cilantro 1 cup
- Hot cooked rice
- Flour tortillas 8 inches

xxxxxxxxxxxxxxxxxxxxxxxxxxxxxxxxxxxxxxxxxxxx

Procedure:

1. Take an electric pressure cooker and sauté its setting on 6 qt size in. and adjust it in on high heat.

2. Add the oil, in some batches, sauté the carrot, pork, onion, and also garlic until it gets golden brown.

3. Return all the items to the pressure cooker.

4. Add the enchilada sauce, jalapeno, water, and cilantro.

5. Lock up the lid, close the pressure–release valve.

6. Adjust it to high heat for 30 minutes.

7. Let it release naturally for 10 minutes.

8. Quick the release of any remaining pressure.

9. Serve it with rice and tortillas.

10. Serve it immediately and enjoy it.

Recipe 27 - Memphis Style Ribs

This recipe is to make a new version of making dried Memphis ribs. Serve it with smoked paprika, and it becomes more delicious when you make it by grilling on hot coals.

Total Prep Time: 20 min

Yield: 6

List of Ingredients:

- Onion powder 1 tsp.
- Vinegar White ½ cup
- Water 1 by 2 cup
- Smoked paprika 3 tbsp.
- Brunet sugar 2 tbsp.
- Salt by 2 tsp.
- Ground coarsely pepper 2 tsp.
- Concentrate of garlic 1 tsp.
- Cumin ground 1 tsp.
- Mustard ground 1 tsp.
- Thyme dried 1 tsp.
- Oregano dried 1 tsp.
- Salt celery 1 tsp.
- Pepper Cayenne ¾ tsp.
- Pork baby rack back ribs 2 (about 5 lbs.)

xxxxxxxxxxxxxxxxxxxxxxxxxxxxxxxxxxxxxxxxx

Procedure:

1. Take an electric pressure cooker in 6 qt size, combine the water and vinegar, brush it on the ribs, pour the remaining mixture into the cooker.

2. Add and combine the 1 to 12 ingredients together but reserve the half.

3. Sprinkle the ribs with remaining of the half seasoning blend.

4. Cut these ribs into the serving-size pieces and convert them into the pressure cooker.

5. Lock up the lid, close the valve of pressure–release.

6. Adjust it to high heat for about 20 minutes.

7. Let it release naturally for 10 minutes.

8. Quick the release of any residual pressure.

9. Remove the ribs and fat from the cooking juice.

10. Use the clean brush, to brush on the ribs liberally, with the cooking skimmed juices.

11. Sprinkle it using reserved seasoning.

12. Serve the ribs with the remaining juice and immediately let's enjoy it.

Recipe 28 - Cooker Balsamic Chicken and Apple

This recipe has an amazing texture with a sweet and tart flavor, this meal is super quick, and you can easily make it and serve it as the starter.

Total Prep Time: 15 min

Yield: 4

List of Ingredients:

- Juice or apple cider 0.25 cup
- Balsamic vinegar 0.25 cup
- Lemon juice 2 tbsp.
- Pepper 0.5 tsp.
- Garlic powder 0.5 tsp.
- Paprika 0.5 tsp.
- Chicken bone-in thigh 4 (1.5 lbs.) skin removed
- Dried thyme 0.5 tsp.
- Salt 0.5 tsp.
- Butter 2 tbsp.
- Flour 2 tbsp.
- Chicken broth 0.5 cup

xxxxxxxxxxxxxxxxxxxxxxxxxxxxxxxxxxxxxxxxxxxxxxx

Procedure:

1. Take a small bowl, add and combine 1 to 9 ingredients.

2. Take an electric pressure cooker and place the chicken in 6 qt size. Pour the broth mixture on it.

3. Lock up the lid, close the pressure–release valve.

4. Adjust it to high heat for 10 minutes.

5. Let it release naturally for 10 minutes.

6. Quick the release of any remaining pressure.

7. Remove the chicken and keep it warm; skim the fat from the cooking liquid.

8. Take a small saucepan, melt the butter, add the flour, whisk it until it gets smooth,

9. Add cooking liquid gradually, stir and cook it until sauces become thickened for 2-3 minutes.

10. Serve it with chicken and enjoy it.

Recipe 29 - Cooker Chicken Thighs in Wine Sauce

This recipe has an interesting texture, and everyone would love it if you served it with mashed potatoes and peas. Let's try it now and enjoy it.

Total Prep Time: 20 min

Yield: 4

List of Ingredients:

- Butter 2 tbsp.
- Fresh sliced mushrooms 1 cup
- Chicken thighs bone-in 6, skin removed (about 2¼ lbs.)
- Salt 1/4 tsp.
- Pepper 1/4 tsp.
- Paprika 1/4 tsp.
- All-purpose flour 1/3 cup
- Chicken broth 1/2 cup
- White wine 1/2 cup
- Italian seasoning 1/4 tsp.
- thinly sliced green onion 3

xxxxxxxxxxxxxxxxxxxxxxxxxxxxxxxxxxxxxxxxxxxx

Procedure:

1. Take an electric pressure cooker to select the sauté setting on 6-qt for medium heat.

2. Now add 1 tbsp. butter slowly.

3. When it becomes hot, add the mushrooms, cook it until it gets tender for 3 to 4 minutes.

4. Remove it and sprinkle the chicken with pepper, salt, paprika, and Italian seasoning.

5. Take the shallow bowl and place the flour, add the chicken a few pieces at a time and toss to coat it, and shake off its excess.

6. Heat the leftover butter in the pressure cooker, brown the chicken from both sides.

7. Remove it and add the broth and wine to the pressure cooker.

8. Cook, it for 2-3 minutes, stir it in the loosened browned bits from the pan.

9. Now press the cancel.

10. Return to the chicken and mushrooms in the cooker and add green onion.

11. Lock up the lid, close the pressure–release valve.

12. Adjust it to high heat for 10 minutes.

13. Let it release naturally for 10 minutes.

14. Quick the release of any remaining pressure.

15. A thermometer should be inserted into the chicken, and its reading will be at least 165°F.

16. Serve it immediately and enjoy your meal.

Recipe 30 - Cooker Cheery - Almond Oatmeal

This recipe is a simple, satisfying, and sweet dish, and you can serve it as breakfast. It's a quick dish to make and have fun with your breakfast.

Total Prep Time: 12 min

Yield: 6

List of Ingredients:

- Ground cinnamon 1/2 tsp.
- Dried cherries 1 cup
- almond Vanilla milk 4 cups
- oats Steel-cut 1 cup
- brown sugar Packed 1/3 cup
- Salt 1/2 tsp.
- Optional: additional vanilla milk

xxxxxxxxxxxxxxxxxxxxxxxxxxxxxxxxxxxxxxxxxxxxx

Procedure:

1. Take a pressure cooker in the 6 qt size, coat it using cooking spray and combine 1 to 6 ingredients.

2. Lock up the lid, close the valve of pressure–release.

3. Adjust it to high heat for about 12 minutes.

4. Let it release naturally for around 10 minutes.

5. Quick the release of any residual pressure.

6. Now serve it with the extra almond milk (only if you want)

7. Serve it immediately and enjoy it.

About the Author

From a young age, Zoe loved being in the kitchen! More specifically, her uncle's bakery. Despite not actually working there, she would sit on the working table and watch herself get covered in flour over the next couple of hours. She also watched closely as her uncle kneaded the dough, measured out ingredients, and even decorated cakes. Even though she never tried doing it herself, she could recite the steps to most of the baked goods sold like her favorite song.

It wasn't until her 16th birthday, though, that she realized just how much she wanted to dedicate her life to making desserts too. No matter how much Zoe's mom insisted on buying a beautiful cake from a local bakery for her Sweet 16 party, Zoe wouldn't budge. She wanted to make the cake herself, and she did. Even though it wasn't the prettiest of cakes, it tasted delicious! Her whole family still remembers the flavor combo to this day: pistachio and orange cake. From there, things only got better!

After graduating from culinary school, Zoe worked in some of the finest bakeries throughout Europe. She wanted to learn from the best. Eventually, however, she decided to go back home and start her own business in Chicago, near her friends and family. That business is now one of the nicest bakeries in the city, which she has run with the help of her best friend, Lola, since 2015

Author's Afterthoughts

Hi there!

This is me trying to thank you for supporting my writing by purchasing my cookbook. I can't begin to express how much it means to me! Even though I've been doing this for quite a while now, I still love to know that people enjoy making my recipes, and I like to thank them for it personally.

You see, without you, my job would be meaningless. A cook with no one to eat their food? A cookbook author with no one to read their book? I need you to love my work to be rewarding, so do you?

One of the biggest ways to thank you for supporting me is by asking what you like or dislike most about my books. Are the recipes easy to follow? Do you think I should write more baking books, or what would you like to see more of? I will get to your suggestions for new books and improvements soon, ready to use them for my next book — so don't be shy!

THANK YOU.

ZOE MOORE

Printed in Great Britain
by Amazon